WISDOM SEEKS HER WAY

Liberating The Power of Women's Spirituality

Maria Riley, OP

Center of Concern
Washington, D.C.
1987

Copyright ©1987 by Center of Concern
ISBN 0934255-04-0

All rights reserved. No part of this book may be reproduced by any means and in any form whatsoever without written permisson from the publisher.

Center of Concern
3700 13th Street, NE
Washington, D.C. 20017

Book Design: Center for Educational Design and Communication
Cover Design: Cindy Fowler

Contents

SERIES PREFACE — i

ACKNOWLEDGEMENTS — iv

WHY WOMEN'S SPIRITUALITY? — 1

PROCESS — 8

SESSIONS
    Gathering — 11
    Wholeness/Brokenness — 17
    Bodyspirit — 27
    Relationships — 39
    Work — 49
    Leisure — 59
    Transformation — 69

RESOURCES — 78

CENTERING EXERCISES — 80

GROUP FACILITATION — 82

RESPONSE — 83

SERIES PREFACE

Energies for Social Transformation

At the beginning of the cosmos: the unleashing of unbelievable energy. Energy expanding through spaces and periods of time that stretch the limits of human imagining. Energy, the dynamism of life, generating creativity and hope. Energy, the vibrant soul of all that is and is becoming. An active name for God.

The universe and all of human life have been shaped and reshaped by the interweaving flows of energies over eons. Human history and contemporary society are the legacy of the convergences and clashes of those energies.

How can the energies, flowing within us, around us, among us, be guided to create a more liberating, just, and loving human community–the kind of world Jesus and the women and men who shared community with him envisioned when they spoke of the coming of the Reign of God?

That question is at the heart of this series of small books from the CENTER OF CONCERN. **Energies for Social Transformation** is being designed to help individuals and groups get in touch with the deepest human/divine energies within them, among them, around them in society. We hope it will facilitate the discernment of the action and call of God, and free those energies for the task of social transformation required if God is to reign more fully over human life and we are to know a societal life graced with greater justice and love.

The idea for the series emerged out of a variety of concerns shared by CENTER staff. Social transformation for a more just society is a massive undertaking. We have watched the energy and commitment to change that set the 1960's on fire in the U. S. co-opted or bottled up in the frustration and disillusionment of the 1970's, dissolving all too often into cynical disillusionment in the 1980's. Conspicuous radicals of the 60's have emerged as establishment neo-conservatives in the 80's, speaking of their "conversions" and praising the system that is now treating them so well. Even those who did not succumb to such "conversions" saw many in their ranks suffer burn-out.

Through these decades the realization has gradually grown that institutional social change not grounded in cultural renewal is too shallow. The myths, the values, the images, the hopes, the dreams of a people—these give guidance to human energies. If the injustices they embody are not cleansed, if they are not broken open and reshaped, societal progress will continue to be undermined and eroded—like the biblical mansion built on sand. The reign of God demands both institutional and cultural transformation.

That challenge can only be taken up in any sustained way by people who can draw upon the energies, rootedness, and staying power of communities of faith. Rich community life is essential for providing the love and cohesion necessary for true conversion, creative re-visioning, and faithful commitment to social transformation in the spirit of Jesus.

The Second Vatican Council generated an important renewal of faith, community life, and Christian spirituality which have begun to give birth to this essential context. There have been some serious limitations in this renewal, however, limitations that must be overcome if the energies of God flowing within and among us are to be really liberated to serve the emergence of God's Reign in society.

In the renewal in spirituality flowing out of the Council, for example, the principal channels of growth have been opened by psychology. Psychological insights have opened our eyes in remarkable ways to God's presence and movement in the emotional energies of our interior lives. But they have been far less successful in helping us meet and be renewed by the God of political and economic, social and cultural life who was the heart and focus of Israel's faith.

This limitation has unwittingly re-enforced the Enlightenment compartmentalization of life that has locked Christian faith in the realm of private life. The God of unbounded cosmic energy, however, will not be domesticated. We are being called to liberate our faith energies, to reintegrate in a single faith vision all of our life commitments, all dimensions of personal and social life. **Energies for Social Transformation** hopes to nurture that reintegration.

Another significant discovery during the post-Vatican II renewal has been the gradual realization that the experience and energies of some groups have been overlooked, ignored, rejected as insignificant. The women of the world are among these groups. So are the poor. God's Reign cannot be whole until they are liberated and integral participants in a just and loving human community. Volumes in this series are designed to enable their voices to be heard and their energies liberated in some small way for the social transformation that is needed to redeem us all.

It is ironic that in an era when we know more about the energies of the cosmos than ever before and when we can release and guide more power than ever before, our culture engenders so much passivity and paralysis. **Energies for Social Transformation** is offered as a help to breaking out of that paralysis, to discovering the divine energies moving in society, and to entering with compassionate justice and fierce love into the redeeming of the earth.

–James E. Hug, SJ

•••

ACKNOWLEDGEMENTS

Wisdom Seeks Her Way

This book's process began in 1984 when the National Sisters Vocation Conference asked me to give a presentation at their annual meeting. They gave me the title "Feminine Consciousness: Naming our Reality." Working with the content of that title presented me with an enduring challenge as well as the desire to respond to its call. At the conference I said, "What do we know because we are women? This topic has started me on a journey of exploration of which I share some of the tentative steps with you. I share them with you with great confidence because you are carriers of women's consciousness...This presentation is only the beginning of the exploration of women's consciousness and its creative power for the future. I invite you to join in this exploration and in the power of our cumulative womanhood and all that it means by beginning with yourself."

This book is the fruition of three years' reflection, research and dialogue with many women and some men along the way. Its format remains true to my original insight: Women are the carriers of a consciousness that holds promise for transforming our world and our church to be more whole and holy. But we need to reflect consciously upon our experience and discover its meaning if the power of women's wisdom is to be liberated. So this book is an invitation to participate in a process involving both personal reflection and sharing with other women as we seek to articulate our wisdom and bring its power to bear on our world.

WISDOM SEEKS HER WAY has been born through the efforts of many women. The women who have been part of the Center of Concern during these years were the primary community who tested, tasted and struggled with the early interviews and group reflection processes: Candy Warner, Jane Blewett, Mary Jo Woltman, Shirley Edwards, Khanh Bui, Sylvia Diss, Lisa Sosa and Emily Schwartz. The women, rich and diverse in experience and culture, who participated in the 1985 Center of Concern Sabbatical, stretched the boundaries of the process: Dolores Brinkel, Patrice Coolick, Ruth Egar,

Lourdes Fernandez, Marianna Halsmer, Cathy Rowe, Mary Carol Schroeder, Pat Sealy and Elizabeth Mkame.

During 1985 and 1986 the process was piloted in several different settings of women and each time the willingness of the women to enter into an evolving process and to critique it honestly enriched and focused my work. I am particularly grateful to the women who participated in a retreat at Marianist Apostolic Center in Glenco, Missouri, the women and few men who participated in a day's workshop during Institute '86 at St.-Mary-of-the-Woods College in Terra Haute, Indiana, and to the women who participated in two retreat days in 1986 and 1987 at the Institute Mission and Ministry in Paterson, New Jersey.

Special recognition and appreciation go to Nanette Cormier, a research assistant at the Center of Concern from September 1985 through December 1986. Nan entered into the process as co-creator, organizer, interviewer, reflector and writer. She developed many of the preliminary materials and was intimately involved with the process until she left in December, 1986. Her wit and wisdom are woven throughout.

Kit Collins, Melanie Guste, Angela Marney, and Mavi Coakley of the Center for Educational Design and Communication, Washington, DC, were the midwives for the process and the book. Their enthusiasm and creative critiques have shaped the process as you now see it. They brought form and beauty to the content. I am grateful to them.

I am also grateful to the Society of the Sacred Heart Fund for Ministry, the Special Needs Fund of the Sisters of Loretto, and the North American Province of the Xaverian Brothers whose grants have partially funded this work.

Final and special appreciation goes to my colleagues at the Center of Concern. Their constant affection and support, as well as their serious review of my efforts, continue to sustain me in my work. Special appreciation goes to Anne Hope, George Ann Potter and Jim Hug who were the final readers of the process and to David Simmons who graciously provides the technical and logistical backup to all our work.

•••

woman spirit

Why Women's Spirituality?

ERA, pay equity, "feminization of poverty," sexual harassment, reproductive rights, "take back the night," ordination of women, mutuality of women and men in the home and in the workplace, sexism, feminism—these words and the ideas they symbolize would have carried no meaning for most people some 25 years ago. They illustrate in a small way the profound social, cultural shift that is going on in the United States, as well as across the world, as the women's movement continues to evolve and develop during the final quarter of the 20th century. Few social historians recording the early activities of the movement, often with a trivializing note, foresaw the potential reverberations it would bring through all human systems and structures, from the personal to the global.

Because "womanspirit rising" is one of the most dynamic "signs of our times" with such far-reaching consequences for the quality of human life in the future, it deserves serious attention. Its foundational belief rests on women's conciousness of our birthright as persons of equal dignity, potential and worth with men. The movement seeks that this birthright be recognized not only in rhetoric but in structures and social systems. This recognition brings into question all structures and systems where women find themselves excluded, ignored, trivialized or marginated. It challenges time-honored customs or beliefs which identify women as dependent, deficient or devious. It touches the dynamics of relationships between women and men everywhere, within the family structure, in the workplace, in the church. It denies the legitimacy of patriarchy, that belief and system which declares man to be superior to woman and therefore the rightful ruler of the church and the society. It also demands change.

FROM EQUALITY TO TRANSFORMATION

However, as the woman's movement matures the question of what kind of change is needed becomes central. Early efforts, shaped by an analysis of the basic inequality of women and men in the church and society, concentrated on creating for women equal opportunity and access to the public world dominated by men. While not abandoning these goals, more and more women are questioning the validity of the shape, dynamics, agendas and values of the patriarchal world. Not only the structural exclusion of women is questioned but the very cultural imperatives by which the male-directed world operates are being challenged.

For many women the agenda has moved beyond equality to the transformation of social structures and systems that would recognize the full and equal humanity of all persons, women/men, Black/White/Hispanic/Indian/Asian, young/old, the differently-abled. This transformation must also include the present structure of relationship between countries of the North and the South as well of between the East and the West. The demand for equality remains but it is understood as a demand for a more equal world for all. The questions then become what kind of world – and church – are we seeking and what do we as women bring to the process of transformation?

THE RISING OF THE WOMEN

"Bread and Roses," a rallying song for the movement, asserts "the rising of the women means the rising of the race." Many argue that if women had more decision-making power, the world and the church would be different. Carol Gilligan's ground-breaking work IN A DIFFERENT VOICE presents empirical data showing that women do have different sets of developmental experiences that bring them to values and perspectives that are different from men's. Many women feel intuitively that they operate out of different categories than most men and have experiences to verify that intuition. We are also confronted with the traditional list of feminine and masculine qualities which are highly suspect. Those very categories have been used to legitimate the definition of women – and men – that forces them into role expectations that not only the women's movement and modern psychology, but also personal experience, repudiate.

What then do women bring to the process of transformation? And from where does this power and energy arise? These two questions have guided the development of the process of this book. How can we come into contact with our spirituality as women? Where do we begin to move beyond some general language about women's spirituality into a deeper personal understanding of our particular life/faith experience as well as women's life/faith experience? How can we begin to articulate that spirituality and discover in it the energy for transformation of ourselves, our church and our world to be more human, whole and holy?

THE AUTHORITY OF EXPERIENCE

Women's experience is the authentic touchstone to naming our own spirituality. Historically our religious tradition has been interpreted, celebrated, liturgized and articulated by men. Our God language and images have been primarily masculine. To make this observation is not so much to say that the articulation of our faith is wrong as to say that it is incomplete and distorted. It does not represent the full image of God as Genesis 1:27 teaches: God created humanity, male and female, in the image of God.

To move beyond the incompleteness and distortions it is necessary to bring women's experience and voice into dialogue with the prevailing traditions. But such a challenge demands that women take their experience seriously enough to discover and authenticate its truth. It is a process of separating out, in Anne Wilson Schaef's categories, (1) what we've been told, from (2) what we believe, from (3) what we **know** from our own experience. It is in this final stage, when we can articulate what we **know**, in that Biblical sense of the unity of experience, feeling and thought, that we begin to discover our truth.

FROM EXPERIENCE TO MEANING

While personal experience is the authentic starting point in the process of discovering our spirituality, it is not an end in itself. We need to move within the experience in search of its meaning, for us personally as well as for others. We need to discover that all dimensions of life are revelatory of God. In that discovery we will begin to recognize God's continuing presence and revelation in all of life, in nature, in our relationships, in the joy, sorrows, conflicts and celebrations that shape the dailiness of our individual lives, and in the larger social, political and economic realities of our time.

God's presence and revelation amid all life's processes is not immediately apparent. To discover it requires that we cultivate a consciousness that continues to seek meaning—God's meaning—within the events of our lives. In this search, women's experience is particularly important because it often calls into question the dualisms that shape our traditional view of the holy: sacred/secular, spirit/body, contemplation/action, church/world and spiritual/natural.

These dualisms have inhibited our ability to recognize the sacred in the secular, our body as the incarnation of our spirit, the church as part of the world. They have tried to limit the presence and action of God to a very narrow range of human experience. Could this be the reason so many women do not think of themselves as having a spirituality? Furthermore the dualisms have clouded our realization that we, by our very lives, give shape to God's on-going creative presence and continuing revelation in human history. We also have the power to inhibit God's activity.

FROM THE PERSONAL TO THE COMMUNAL

Each of our life experiences is uniquely personal. No one set of experiences can become the norm for "women's experience." We are too different in background, culture, race, ethnic history, personality type, class. At times we are at odds with each other, set against each other by political, economic, social or religious structures. Life has treated us differently.

The question is, are there any commonalities even amidst the differences? Do these commonalities begin to repeat themselves to form patterns of meaning and insight? By bringing our personal experience into dialogue with other women's experience can we begin to discover both what is unique and what is shared? Through this process can we begin to act out of the authority of our shared understandings to struggle for the transformation of both the church and the world to be more holy, whole and human?

DIALOGUE WITH OUR TRADITIONS

This project begins with the assumption that the participants are part of a faith tradition. My own is Roman Catholic. It is also assumed that all faith traditions carry much wisdom and grace as well as sinfulness in their history. Churches, like individuals, are always in need of conversion. Today many women are calling their churches beyond patriarchy and the sinful structures and attitudes of diminishment of women that it perpetuates.

For many women the discovery of patriarchy and its accompanying sexism within their religious tradition has brought profound anger and grief. Some have felt that, in conscience, they must reject a tradition that denies their very personhood as a woman.

But others are called, in conscience, to labor with their faith tradition to bring forth an ever more transparent image of the God of our mothers and fathers, who created woman and man in the image of the divine. Such a task demands that we labor to understand how our experience as women is revelatory of God. Out of this understanding we must then enter into dialogue with our faith tradition, challenging its patriarchal structure and theology. In the dialogue the community of believers, bearers of the wisdom and grace of the tradition, will protect us from our own egoism and eccentricities as we search together for the truth that will "make us free."

THE PROCESS OF OUR TASK

The initial demand of our process toward transformation is to honor our own experience as women. This book and its process are offered as an invitation to get in touch with our personal experiences and to share those reflections with other women in search of our truth. The process has three movements: personal reflection around experience, shared reflection and movement toward transformation.

Personal Reflection

The process is divided into seven sessions: gathering, wholeness/brokenness, bodyspirit, relationships, work, leisure and transformation. For each section you are asked to spend some time in personal reflection and response–prose, poetry, sketching, imaging. Before you begin each reflection period, spend some time relaxing and centering yourself (see page 80).

The questions offered are suggestions and you should feel free to respond to them in any way you want. During this part of the process try to stay very close to your feeling responses because they are the touchstones that help us to understand the meaning of the experience in our lives. Take time to bless your experience for the revelation it has given you.

Shared Reflection

The time of sharing your experience with others is a sacred time for you are entering into the mystery of God in each other's lives. Honor that sanctuary. In the group sharing you will be exploring each other's understandings and searching for common threads and patterns as well as recognizing differences. As a group you may have to develop a delicate discipline among yourselves to allow the freedom for differences to emerge. You may have to remind yourself, and each other, that the purpose of the group is to share experiences and insights, not to debate the "correctness" of these insights. At times the group will want to reflect upon those insights in the light of their faith tradition to call forth further understanding both of the tradition and the new insights. At times the group will want to reflect on its own process and feeling responses, to understand its own growth. Ideally, the group should be no more than four or five, to allow sufficient time for sharing within a reasonable time frame (see page 82 for suggestions on group facilitation).

Transformation

Implicit in this process is the belief that women's experience and the wisdom that flows from that experience has power to transform the structures of the church and the society beyond patriarchy. It has the power to bring new dimensions of understanding and response to the profound problems that plague our age: war, terrorism and torture, starvation, poverty, abuse of power, ecological destruction, nuclear threat.

As women become more secure in the wisdom and power of their insights, both individually and collectively, we will know a greater freedom to speak our truth and to live our lives out of that truth. This personal transformation becomes a resource for transformation of life around us, from the personal/relational to the political/economic and the ecclesial.

SPIRITUALITY

Throughout this introduction, as well as throughout the period of 18 months in which I developed this process in collaboration with many different women, I have specifically avoided defining spirituality. I have done so purposely because I believe that we as women must search for our own spirituality – our own spirit. For too long a time we have been told what our spirituality is, mostly by male clergy, preachers, theologians or spiritual directors. The whole thesis of this process is that our spirituality flows from our experience and what we have learned from our experiences.

From this point of view, spirituality is not something we have or we don't have. Spirituality is a life process. It is coming in touch with our unique spirit, as lived through our life experiences. It is the process whereby we recognize the God of our experiences as well as the God of our faith tradition. It is the process of searching for our authentic voice so that we can speak with the authority that our experience has given us.

Our spirituality takes shape in the quality of our relationships, with ourselves, with others, with all of creation, and with God. These relations continue to lead us toward the recognition of how profoundly social and relational the whole and holy human person is. And how profoundly social and relational God is.

Out of this rich vision and experience, we are energized for the task of transformation of our church and our world.

•••

Process

- Gather a group of 4 or 5 women who are interested in reflecting on their spirituality.
- Begin the process with the **Gathering** section of the book.
- Plan when you will meet again. Where, when, who will facilitate, who will prepare a short prayer or ritual?
- Before meeting again, each participant is asked to spend a period of time reflecting on the next section of the book.

PERSONAL REFLECTION

The following process is recommended:
- Spend some time centering yourself. (See page 80).
- Read slowly through all the questions.
- As you begin to recall experiences, stay very close to your feeling responses.
- Respond in whatever way you want—poetry, prose, sketches, etc. on the **Reflection** pages in your book. Enjoy yourself.
- Take some time to pray for Wisdom and bless your experience.

GROUP REFLECTION

The following process is recommended:
- Spend some time relaxing and centering yourselves.
- Take a few quiet minutes for each person to recall her own reflections.
- Then each woman is invited to share whatever she would like of her personal reflections.
- The group will then pause to think about what they have heard.
- Consider the questions offered as discussion starters for the group as you begin to explore the meaning of your experiences as women.
- A reflection page is offered for each to note what is important to her.
- Conclude the discussion with a general summary of significant insights. Each woman is invited to contribute.
- Close the session with some form of prayer or ritual.

Sessions

Gathering
Wholeness/Brokenness
Bodyspirit
Relationships
Work
Leisure
Transformation

Gathering

The day of my spiritual awakening was the day I saw and knew I saw all things in God and God in all things.

— Mechtild

Because "womanspirit rising" is one of the most dynamic "signs of our times" with such far-reaching consequences for the quality of human life in the future, it deserves serious attention.

Spirit

*And so I prayed,
and understanding
was given me;*

*I entreated,
and the spirit of Wisdom
came to me.*

*I esteemed her
more than power
and might;*

*Compared with her,
I held riches
as nothing.*

Wisdom 7:7-8

**Use this first session to get to know each other
and to discuss the introduction to the book
as well as the process for exploring
your spirituality as women.**

PEOPLE
    Take time for each woman to introduce herself by telling why she is interested in participating in this process.

PURPOSE
    Take some quiet time to read the introduction "Why Women's Spirituality?"

What did you find most interesting or challenging in the introduction?

Did any questions occur to you?

How do you want to resolve them?

energy

Are there any ideas you do not understand or do not agree with?

PROCESS
   Take some time to discuss the "Process" as outlined on page 8.
   Plan the next session.

Where will it be?

Who will facilitate the group for the session?

Who will plan a short prayer or ritual to bring the group together and to close the session?

Suggestions for facilitation are outlined on page 82.
Several books on women's spirituality and
additional support materials are recommended in the Resource section.

Wholeness

Brokenness

Do you wish to know my meaning?

Then lie down in the fire and breathe

**Women's experience
is the authentic touchstone
to naming our own spirituality.**

counsellor

comfort

*I have determined
to have Wisdom share my life,
knowing she would be my counsellor
in prosperity,
my comfort in cares and sorrow.*

Wisdom 8:9

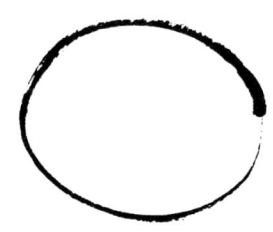

Recall a time in your life when you felt particularly
connnected, balanced or whole.

Feel yourself back into that experience.

What was it like? What was important in it?

What was the source of the contentment?

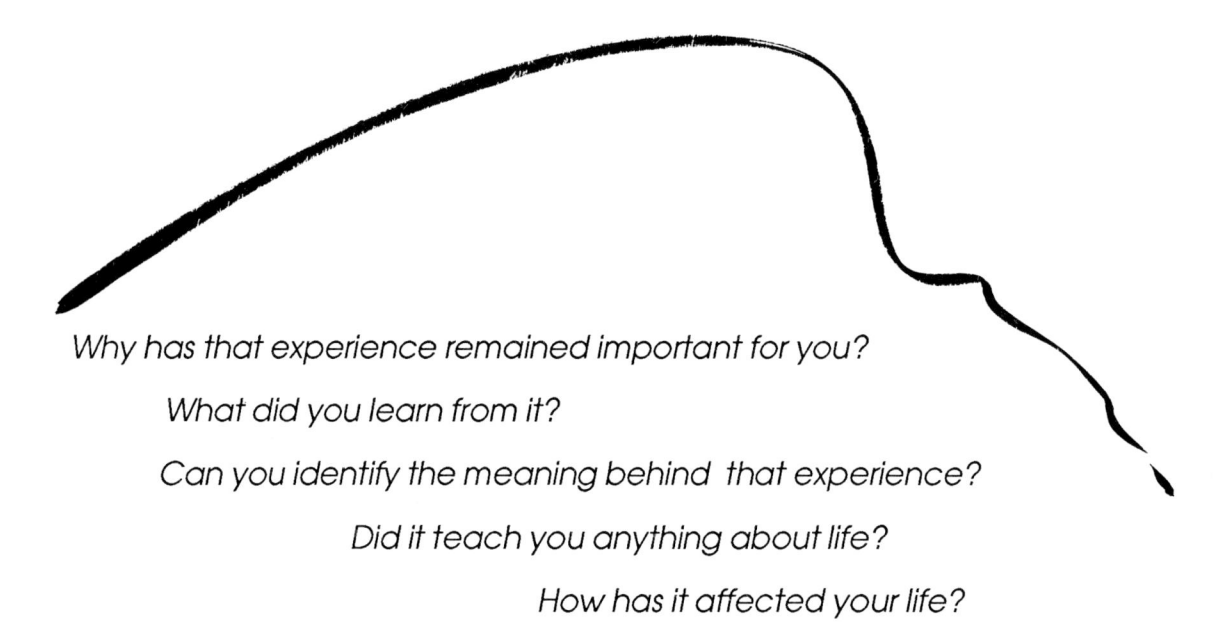

Why has that experience remained important for you?

What did you learn from it?

Can you identify the meaning behind that experience?

Did it teach you anything about life?

How has it affected your life?

Did the experience seem religious to you? If so, how?

Does it now?

Does the experience suggest any new images or names of God to you?

What are they? Are you comfortable with them? Why or why not? Any new images or notions of sin?

Of grace?

Are there stories or images that help you interpret the experience? From where do they come? Scripture, poetry, dance, theology, physics, nature, creation, etc.?

Do you think the experience and your response was shaped by the fact you are a woman?

How?

These reflection questions may also help to illumine an experience that was traumatic for you. Move with your spirit.

Reflections

Group Sharing

  To begin, take some time to recall your personal reflections. What would you like to share with the group about those reflections?

  After the members of the group have shared their personal reflections, take some time to ponder what you have heard.

Do you recognize any common threads or patterns in these experiences? What are they? Do they reveal any new insights or understandings about wholeness/holiness–or brokenness–from woman's experience?

Are you discovering differences to be explored? What are they? What are their roots? *(Remember, the purpose of this conversation is to share experiences and insights, NOT to debate the "correctness" of these insights.)*

Do any images or stories come to your mind that help you interpret the dialogue? Where do they come from: scripture, poetry, nature, etc? What other resources help interpret the significance of the dialogue?

How do you nurture these insights? Does your church experience help you? If so, how? If not, why not?

What is your feeling response to this dialogue? From where is it coming? Compassion, discovery, energy, joy, anxiety, fear, anger? What does your response tell you?

Notes

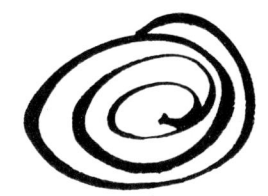

Body Spirit

When, O when will you SOAR on the wings of your LONGING to the blissful heights?

Mechtild

We need to discover that all dimensions of life are revelatory of God.

*Wisdom's closeness to God
lends luster to her noble birth,
since the God of All
has loved her.*

Wisdom 8:3

luster

When did you first

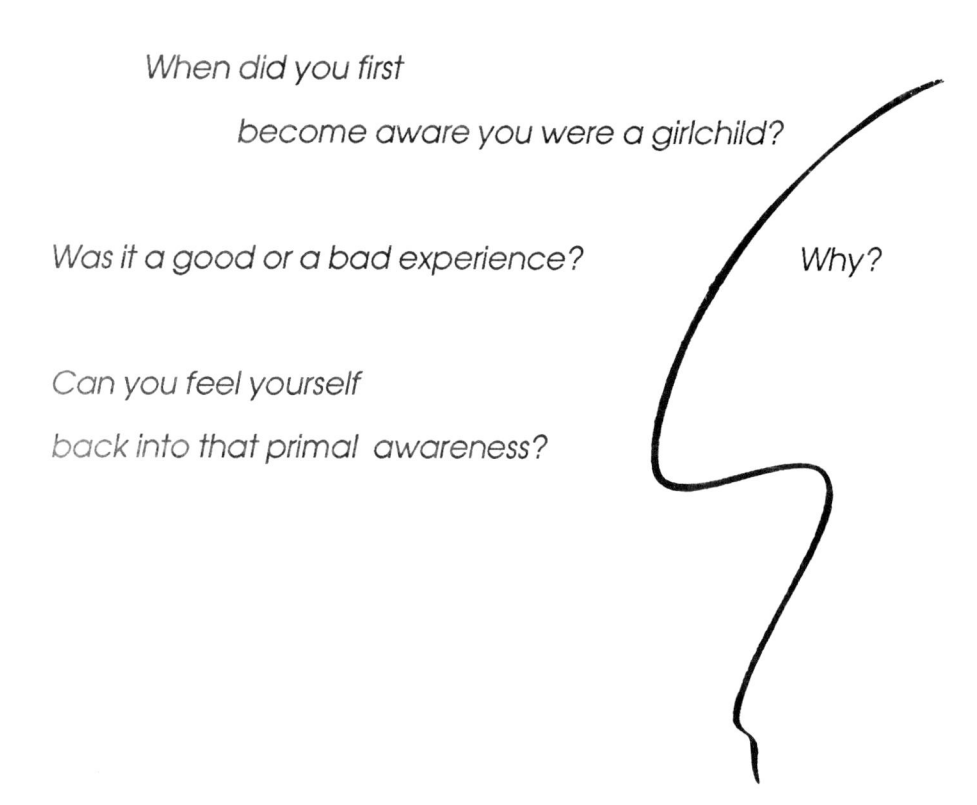

become aware you were a girlchild?

Was it a good or a bad experience?   Why?

*Can you feel yourself
back into that primal awareness?*

*What were some vivid experiences
of being a girl/woman during your adolescent years?*

Were they good or bad experiences?

Did you enjoy those years?   If not, why not?   If so, why?

Woman

What images come to your mind when you think about woman's body/sexuality?

Are they positive or negative images?

Where did these images come from?
How do you feel about these images?

How do you feel about your body/sexuality?
Why?

How has being a woman shaped your self-identity?
Can you recall an experience that was very formative of your identity as a woman?

Feel yourself back into that experience.
Was it positive or negative?   Explain.

How does your sexuality shape your spirituality?

Is this a comfortable question?

Why or why not?

Does this idea differ from what you've traditionally been taught?

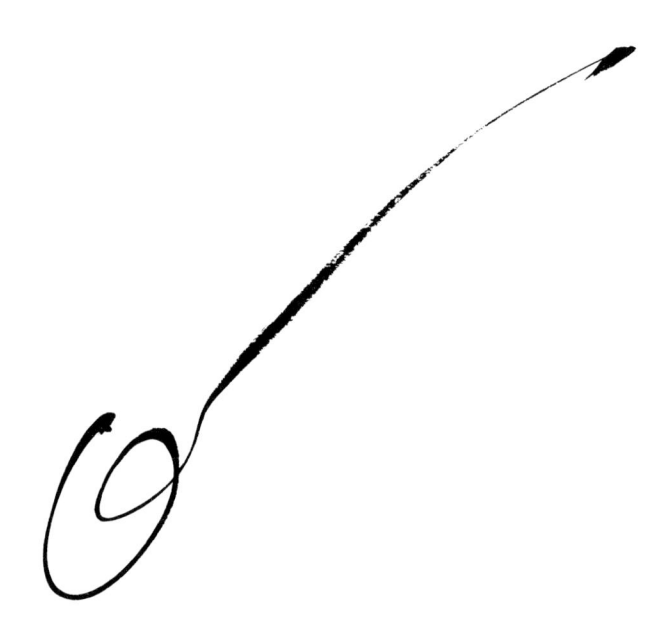

images

What do you think woman's sexuality reveals about God?

What God images does it suggest?
Are you comfortable with those images?

Why or why not?

Reflections

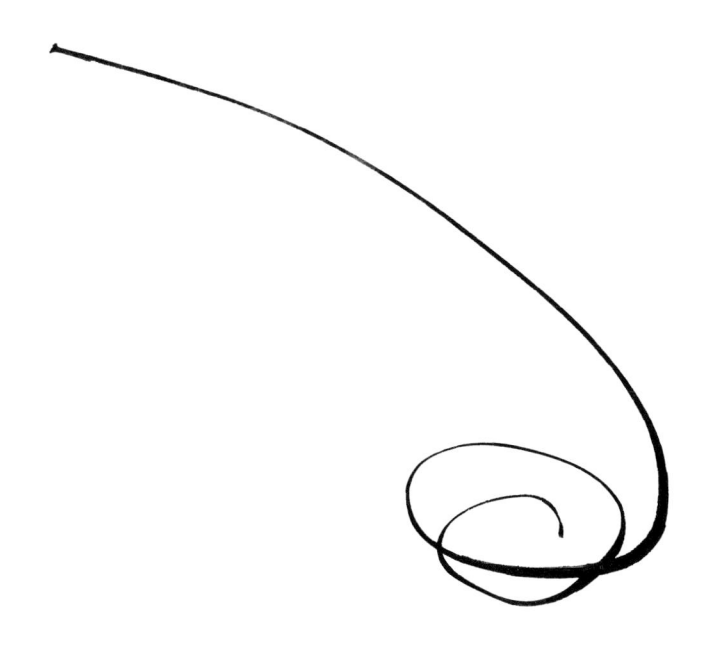

Group Sharing

To begin, take some quiet time to recall your personal reflections. What would you like to share with the group from those reflections?

After the first sharings, take some time to reflect upon what you've heard.

Explore together your positive and negative experiences of being a woman. In your personal life. In the society. In the church.

Can you identify any common threads or patterns in these experiences? What are they. What understandings or new insights do they reveal?

Are there differences you want to explore? What are they? From where do these differences come? Are you comfortable with them? Why or why not?

What word, image or symbol best captures your experience of your sexuality/spirituality, your bodyspirit?

What images of God flow from reflection on women's sexuality/spirituality? Are you comfortable with these images? Explain.

If you had an opportunity to explain your experience of sexuality to the hierarchy of the church, what would you want them to understand?

Has this been a difficult discussion for you as a group? Why? What has been positive for you in the discussion?

Notes

Relationships

God wants to be
known and
loved
through justice
and compassion
julian

> Such a task demands that we
> labor to understand how our experience
> as women is revelatory of God.

Spirituality

*It was Wisdom I loved and
searched for her from my youth.
I resolved to have her as my friend.
I fell in love with her beauty.*

Wisdom 8:2

Connections

Recall an experience when you felt
deeply connected with another
or with others?

Feel yourself back into that experience.
What were the significant parts of that experience?

Disconnections

Recall an experience
when you felt disconnected
and alienated from others?

What was happening in you? In them?
In the relationship?
What has this experience revealed to you about God?
Sin? Grace?

How does the fact that you are a woman shape your relationships?

Does your sexuality enhance or inhibit your relationships?

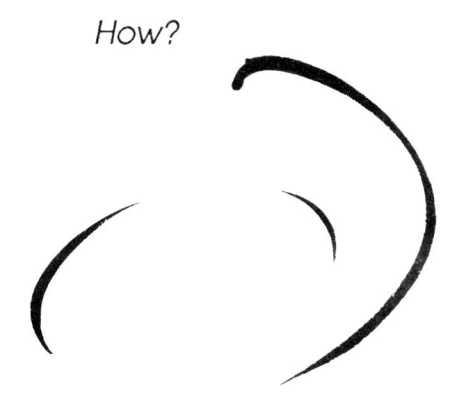

How?

What relationships have brought wholeness, energy, excitement and joy into your life?

What are the characteristics of those relationships?

What images of God do they suggest?

What notions of sin? Grace?
Are these different from what you have been traditionally taught?

How does your experience of solitude interact with your relationships?

Has your experience in relationships given you

a vision for the welfare of the community?

The society?

The human family?

If not, could it?

What difference might it make?

What images of human society might begin to emerge?

Reflections

Group Sharing

Take some quiet time to recall your personal reflections. What do you want to share with the group?

After the initial sharing, take some time to reflect upon what you have heard.

Explore any common themes and patterns you have heard. What new insights or understandings do they reveal to you? About yourself and your relationships?

Did you notice any differences? What are they? From where do these differences arise? Are you comfortable with them? Why or why not?

What do think you women's experience of relationships reveals to us about the meaning of the human family/community? Do you think these insights are presently shaping our political, economic, social or church worlds? Explain.

If they did shape the public world more, what differences would there be?

What do you think women's experience in relationship reveals to us about God's relationship to us? Are there any biblical images or stories that help interpret our experiences in relationships? Are there any images of women in relationships that give us images for God?

Are there any other resources to help you interpret the meaning of our experience of relationships as women?

How are you experiencing this process of reflecting upon the religious meaning of our experiences as women? As an individual? As a group? What do you/we need to do to deepen the experience?

Notes

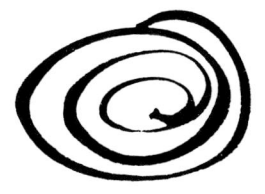

God creates justice in all who will be liberated through goodness

Julian

work

Each of our life experiences
is uniquely personal.
No one set of experiences can
become the norm for "women's experience."

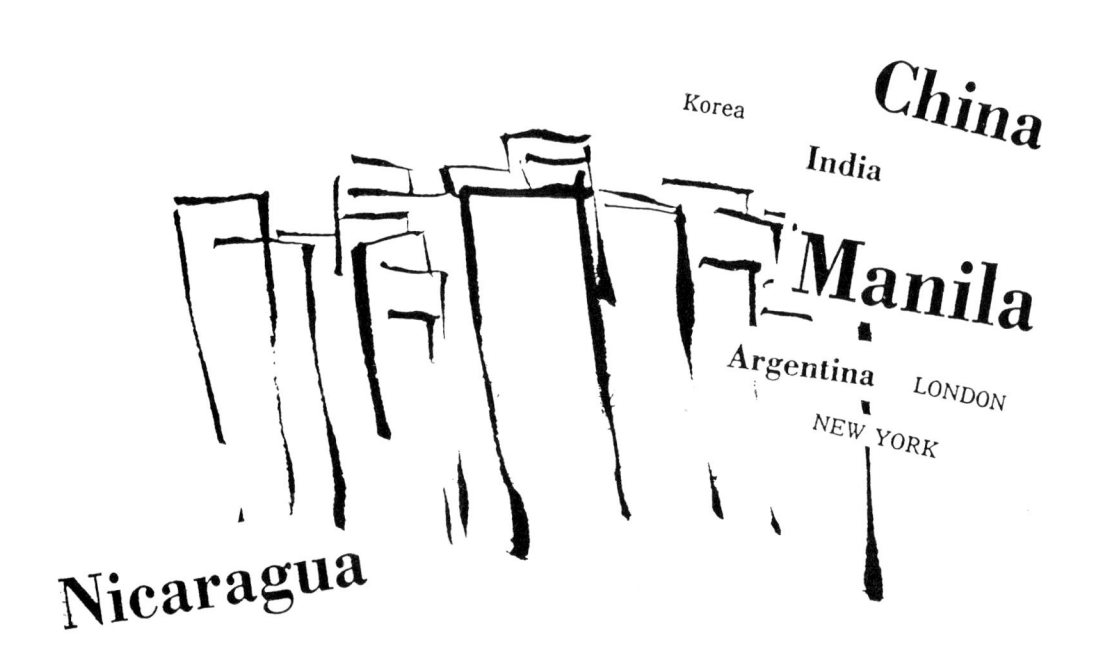

Korea

China

India

Manila

Argentina   LONDON

NEW YORK

Nicaragua

*Yes, Wisdom is an initiate
in the mysteries of God's knowledge,
making choice of the works God is to do.*

Wisdom 8:4

Recall a time when you felt particularly creative, dynamic and full of energy. Where were you? What were you doing? Why was that experience so creative for you?

*Think about your world of work—**all of it**—at home, in the community, voluntary, in your workplace if you work outside your home. What is good and rewarding about your work? Why? What do you find difficult? Why?*

*Do you experience your work
as being creative?
Do you feel that your work
involves you in God's creative
process for human history?
How?*

*If not, why not?
Is the problem in your work?
Or have you not appreciated
your contribution to the human
community?
If not, why not?*

Reflections

Group Sharing

Take some time to quietly recall your personal reflections. What was most significant that you want to bring to the group?

After the initial sharing, take some time to reflect upon what you have heard.

Trace the common threads or patterns you heard. What are they? What understandings or new insights do they reveal?

Are there any differences? What are they? What do they reveal?

How have you experienced your work–ALL OF IT–as women? Have you felt valued? Ignored? Taken for granted? Explain.

How has your work experience shaped your sense of yourself? Your values?

What insights does your experience of work reveal to you about the meaning of work–your work as a woman–"woman's work"–in the human experience? In our society? In the world? About God's on-going creative activity in the world?

Do you feel any tension around this topic? Why? What are its roots? Its history? Talk together beyond these tensions to discover the truth about the value of women's work – for the family, for the church, for the society, for the world.

Notes

Seizure

The fullness of JOY is to behold GOD... in everything.
Julian

**The time of sharing your experience
with others is a sacred time
for you are entering into
the mystery of God in each other's lives.**

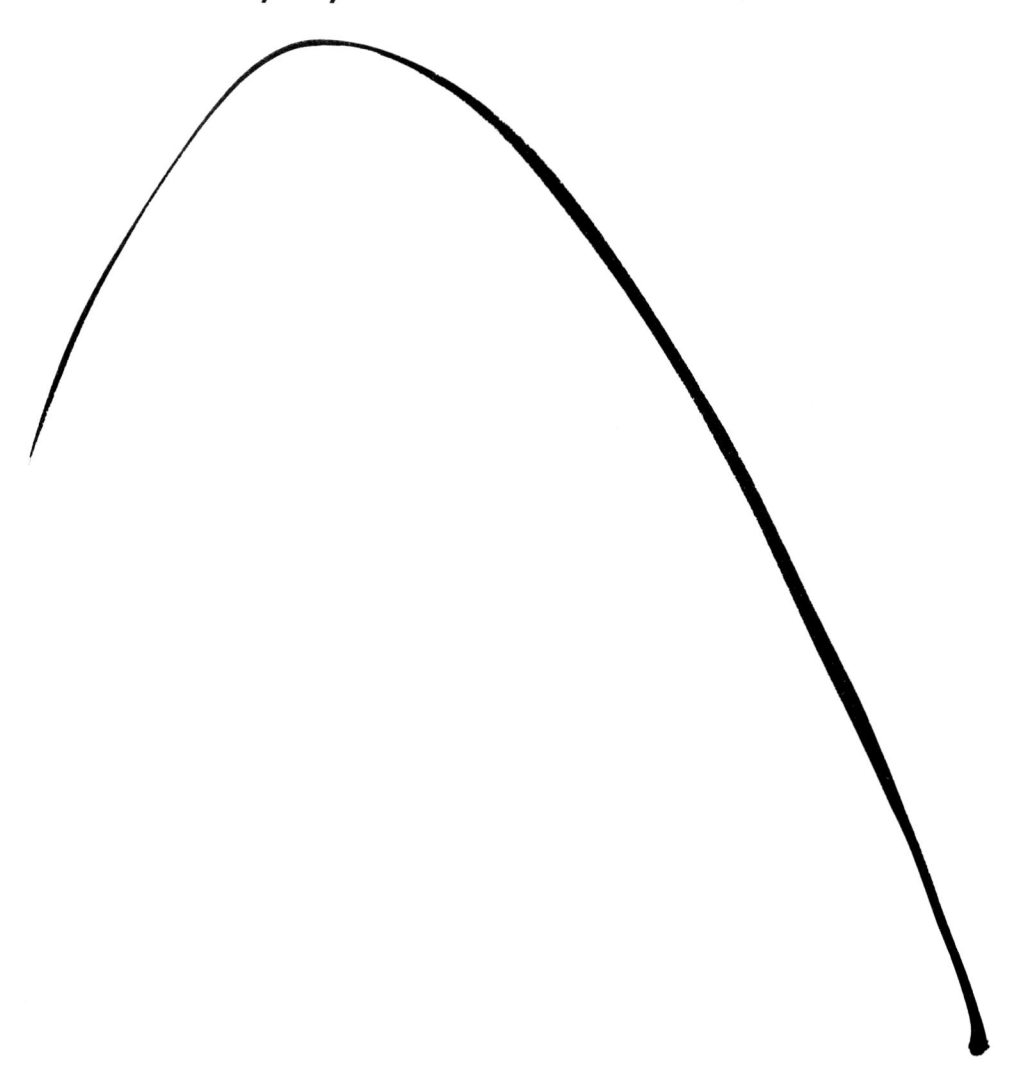

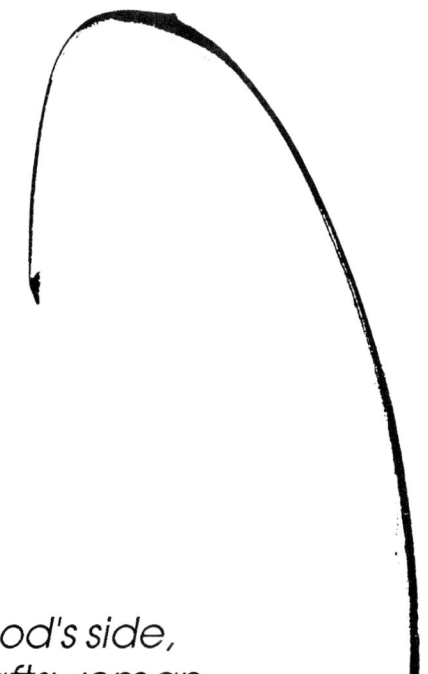

*I was by God's side,
a master craftswoman,
delighting God day after day,
ever at play in God's presence,
at play everywhere in the world,
delighting to be with the children of the earth.*

Proverbs 8:30-31

When was the last time you felt playful? What were you doing?
What was the experience like? Do you often feel playful?
Where, when, with whom do you discover your sense of play?

God

Is physical exercise a part of your day-to-day life?
If so, what form does it take?
How does it make you feel?
Does it make you more aware of your body? Explain.

What other ways do you relax?
What do you enjoy about them?
Why?

Do you ever feel that activities or persons drain energy out of you?
When? What is happening?

Play

How do work and leisure interplay in your life?
    Do you enjoy one more than the other? Why?
        Do you ever think of God as playful?
            Why or why not?
  If so, what images do you have
of God as playful.
    Let your own experience of play lead you.
Are you comfortable with these images?
Why or why not?

Reflections

delighting

Group Sharing

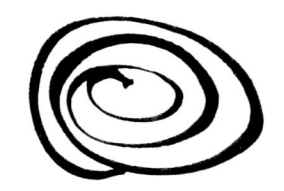

Take some quiet time to recall your reflections. What do you want to share with the group?

After the initial sharing, take some quiet time to reflect upon what you have heard.

Trace the common threads or patterns you heard in these experiences. What are they? What truths or new insights do they reveal?

Explore the differences. What are they? Where do these differences arise?

Are your experiences of playfulness in any way shaped by the fact that you are women? If so how? Can you identify any experiences to support your point?

What do your experiences of play, leisure, creativity and work reveal to you about yourself? About God and God's activity in the world? About the meaning of life? About sin and grace?

What images or stories help you interpret your experience of play, creativity and work? Where do they come from: scripture, poetry, art, nature, etc.? How do they help you understand the meaning of your experiences?

Notes

Transformation

The HOLY SPIRIT flows
through us
with the marvelous
creative POWER
of everlasting
joy!
Mechtild

**The questions then become what kind of world–and church–
are we seeking and what do we as women
bring to the process of transformation?**

*For within Wisdom is a spirit intelligent, holy,
unique, manifold, subtle,
active, incisive, unsullied,
lucid, invulnerable, benevolent, sharp,
irresistible, beneficent,
loving to women and men.*

Wisdom
7:22

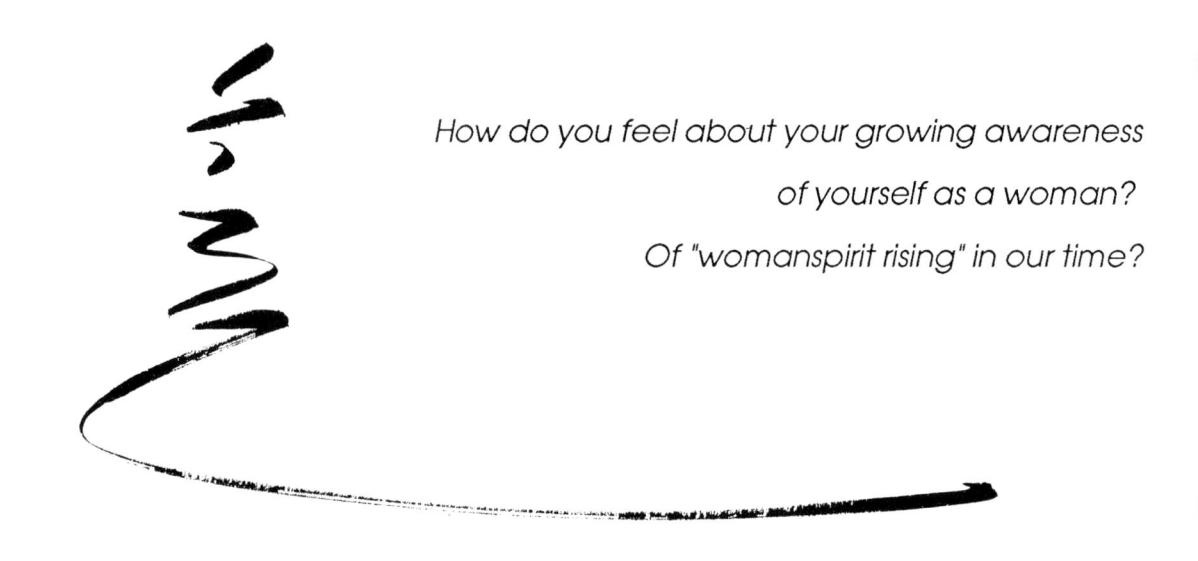

How do you feel about your growing awareness of yourself as a woman? Of "womanspirit rising" in our time?

Do women's experiences and the insights and values flowing from them bring any fresh understandings to your sense of the human person? If so, in what ways? How do they differ from what you have traditionally thought?

Do you think women's experiences

    and the insights and values that flow from them

        bring new understandings and directions

            to address the needs of our time?

If so, in what ways?

    What do you think God is trying to reveal to us,

        to our world, to the church

           through this historical moment

                of woman consciousness and power?

What do you feel is your

contribution to this moment of human history?

Reflections

Group Sharing

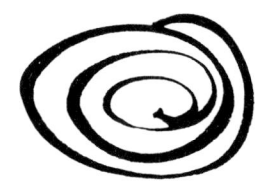

For this final section of the process, take some quiet time and briefly recall the whole process, personal and group sharing. You will probably want to refer to the notes you have taken along the way.

What have you learned through this experience about the meaning and value of your experience as a woman? Does that new knowledge hold power for you? Explain. What images or feelings does it evoke?

What are some of the most important insights about women's spirituality that you have discovered both through your own personal reflection and through the group interaction?

What new images, understandings of God have you experienced through the process? What new notions of sin? And grace? Have they enriched what you have been traditionally taught? Explain.

What can you do to nurture and deepen these insights? What new images of yourself as a woman and of women's potential have come to you?

What are ways that the potential of women's spirituality can be directed toward the transformation of our church and world to greater justice and peace? What do you feel is your contribution?

What word, image, symbol would you want to share as an expression of your spirituality as a woman. How do you feel about it?

What other topics do you think need to be explored?

Notes

Resources

BOOKS

Anthony, Susan B. *SIDEWALK CONTEMPLATIVES.* New York: Crossroads Publishing Company, 1987.

Bankson, Marjory Zoet. *BRAIDED STREAMS.* San Diego, CA: LuraMedia, 1985.

Belenky, Mary Field, Blythe McVicker Clinchy, Nancy Rule Goldberger and Jill Mattuck Tarule. *WOMEN'S WAYS OF KNOWING.* New York: Basic Books, Inc., Publishers, 1986.

Cady, Susan, Marian Ronan and Hal Taussig. *SOPHIA : THE FUTURE OF FEMINIST SPIRITUALITY.* San Francisco: Harper Row Publishers, 1986.

Conn, Joann Wolski (ed.). *WOMEN'S SPIRITUALITY: RESOURCES FOR CHRISTIAN DEVELOPMENT.* New York: Paulist Press, 1986.

Giles, Mary E. (ed.). *THE FEMINIST MYSTIC AND OTHER ESSAYS ON WOMEN AND SPIRITUALITY.* New York: Crossroads Press, 1982.

Ochs, Carol. *WOMEN AND SPIRITUALITY.* Totowa, New Jersey: Rowman and Allanheld, 1983.

FOR PRAYER AND RITUAL

Clarke, Linda, Marian Ronan and Eleanor Walker. *IMAGE BREAKING: IMAGE BUILDING: A Handbook for Creative Worship with Women of Christian Tradition.* New York: The Pilgrim Press, 1981.

Doyle, Brendan, *MEDITATIONS WITH JULIAN OF NORWICH.* Santa Fe, New Mexico: Bear and Company, 1983.

Gjerding, Iben and Katherine Kinnamon (eds.). *NO LONGER STRANGERS: A Resource for Women and Worship.* Geneva, Switzerland: World Council of Churches, 1983.

Johnson, Ann. *MIRYAM OF NAZARETH.* Notre Dame, IN: Ave Maria Press, 1984.

Roller, Karen (ed.). *WOMEN PRAY.* New York: The Pilgrim Press, 1986.

Schaffran, Janet and Pat Kozak. *MORE THAN WORDS: Prayer and Ritual for Inclusive Communities.* Privately Printed. 1986. (Available from Pat Kozak, 1918 West 73rd St., Cleveland, OH 44116).

Woodruff, Sue. *MEDITATIONS WITH MECHTILD OF MAGDEBURG.* Santa Fe, New Mexico: Bear and Company, 1982.

MUSIC

Fulmer, Colleen. *CRY OF RAMAH.* 529 Pomona Ave. Albany, CA 94706. (Tape and music available)

McDade, Carolyn. *RAIN UPON DRY LAND and WE COME WITH OUR VOICES.* 76 Everett Skinner Rd. Plainville, MA 02762. (Tape and music available)

Silvestro, Marsie. *CIRCLING FREE.* Moonsong Productions, 35-16 85th St. 36G, Jackson Heights, NY 11372.

• • •

Centering Exercises

Before beginning each reflection period, both the personal reflection time and the group sharing, take some time to center yourself, to get in touch with your external and internal world.

The following exercises are offered as suggestions. Choose the one or several that best answer your need at the time. You are also encouraged to develop your own centering techniques.

Always begin to relax by finding a comfortable position for you. Put all your concerns aside for the time being and continue to put them aside if they recur during your reflection time.

Breathing
Pay attention to your breathing; slowly breathe in to the count of four or five and breathe out to the count of four or five. Close your eyes and imagine you are inhaling all the freshness and peace of a beautiful day and exhaling all the anxieties and frustrations that surround you. Periodically return to an awareness of the rhythm of your breathing.

Seeing
Look around the room and enjoy the colors and contours that you see. Close your eyes and put your mind in a relaxed state by drawing a wide empty circle; fill the circle with a color that attracted you and let that color recall all the associations – people, places, memories, smells, images – it has for you. Take your time, relax and continue to breathe deeply. The images will come.

Sound
As you are breathing deeply, close your eyes and listen to the sounds around you. Notice the sounds that are outside the room and sounds that are inside the room. Then listen very carefully for any message that you sense is being communicated to you.

Or you may want to spend some time quietly listening to music that you find relaxing while you concentrate on your breathing.

Touch
After you have begun to relax and to breathe deeply, focus your attention on your body – its position, the fabrics and quality of the air that brush against your skin, the contour of the furniture or pillows that support you. Enjoy the sensation of your body.

Relaxing
Stand up and stretch your arms as high above your head as possible. Try to touch the ceiling or sky. Hold that position for a few seconds and then relax. Repeat such stretching and relaxing exercises with other parts of your body. Roll your head and your neck slowly around the top of your spine by dropping your head forward and slowly rolling it to the right. Repeat by rolling it to the left.

Dance
Put on music you respond to. Follow the rhythm with your body movements. Pay particular attention to your body as it flows to the sound of the music.

Speech
As part of your breathing exercises begin to softly repeat a mantra that centers you. A mantra can be any rhythmic sound or phrase that can echo in your memory. Examples include, a letter sound, such as mmmm or oooo or ahhhhh. It can also be words or a prayer from your faith tradition, such as Mercy, Yes, or Come Holy Spirit.

• • •

I am indebted to IMAGE–BREAKING: IMAGE–BUILDING
for some of these centering exercises. See the list of Resources.

Facilitation

The time for sharing personal experience and reflection within the group is a sacred time when you are entering into the mystery of God in each other's lives. Honor that sanctuary. To facilitate each group session, have someone act as group process person.

To assist you in the group process, I offer the following recommendations:

- Take some time for relaxing and centering exercises (see page 80).

- Welcome each woman's participation, but avoid putting anyone on the spot. You may need to invite some members to share their reflections if they do not spontaneously enter the discussion.

- If a woman controls the dialogue or continues to interrupt, remind her that others in the group may want to share insights or complete a thought.

- If the group digresses too widely, summarize the main ideas covered and bring the group back to the focus of the discussion.

- Continue to emphasize the need for mutual respect despite different experiences or understandings. Expressing different points of view often enriches and enlarges our understanding of each other. You do not always have to reach agreement.

- A good way to conclude the group reflection period is to summarize the main points covered. Ask all to contribute to the summary.

- Allow time for prayer.

• • •

Response

      I would like to invite you to respond to the process we have shared through this book. Your response will enhance the process in several ways. It will continue to develop the directing vision of the work: "Women are carriers of a consciousness that holds promise for transforming our world and our church to be more whole and holy." It will also connect us. I will know who you are as you have come to know me through this effort. Finally, you could become a resource for other women in your area who may want to begin the process, if I have the information and the opportunity to connect you.

Please answer these questions briefly.

What was most important for you in this process?

What were some of your most significant insights?

About yourself?

About woman's spirituality?

About God?

About society?

About any of the topics you reflected upon?

Other?

Was the process helpful? What would have made it more helpful?

Would you recommend this book to a friend? Why or why not?

Would you be interested in continuing to participate in a process such as this?

What support materials would be helpful?

What suggestions would you make to improve this book?

*Have you used any other volumes in this series, **Energies for Transformation**? Which ones?*

Any other comments?

Name _____

Address _____

City _____

State _____ Zip _____

I am willing to be contacted by other groups

☐ Yes ☐ No Phone (____) _____

Return to:
Energies for Social Transformation
Center of Concern, Box 101-W
3700 13th Street, NE
Washington, DC 20017